MEASURE ONCE, CUT TWICE

Insights on Life from a Frustrated Woodworker

BILL MILLER

Copyright © 2023 by Bill Miller

MEAUSURE ONCE, CUT TWICE

All rights reserved. No part of this publication may be reproduced, distributed, or transmitted in any form or by any means, including photocopying, recording, or other electronic or mechanical methods, without the prior written permission of the publisher, except in the case of brief quotations embodied in critical reviews and certain other noncommercial uses permitted by copyright law. For permission requests, write to the publisher, addressed "Attention: Permissions Coordinator," at info@beyondpublishing.net

Quantity sales and special discounts are available on quantity purchases by corporations, associations, and others. For details, contact the publisher at the address above.
Orders by U.S. trade bookstores and wholesalers. Email info@BeyondPublishing.net

The Beyond Publishing Speakers Bureau can bring authors to your live event. For more information or to book an event contact the Beyond Publishing Speakers Bureau speak@BeyondPublishing.net

The Author can be reached directly at BeyondPublishing.net
Manufactured and printed in the United States of America distributed globally by BeyondPublishing.net

New York | Los Angeles | London | Sydney

ISBN Hardcover: 978-1-63792-617-8
ISBN Softcover: 978-1-63792-618-5

DISCLAIMER AND/OR LEGAL NOTICES

While all attempts have been made to verify information provided in this book and its ancillary materials, neither the author nor publisher assumes any responsibility for errors, inaccuracies or omissions. Any slights of people or organizations are unintentional. If advice concerning legal or related matters is needed, the services of a qualified professional should be sought.

This book and/or its ancillary materials is not intended for use as a source of legal or accounting advice. Also, some suggestions made in this book and/or its associated ancillary materials concerning referrals, marketing, prospecting, time management, etc., may have inadvertently introduced practices deemed unlawful in certain states and municipalities. You should be aware of the various laws governing business transactions or other business practices in your particular geographical location.

Any references to any persons or businesses, whether living or dead, existing or defunct, is purely coincidental.

TABLE OF CONTENTS

Acknowledgements	7
Preface	8
Introduction:	11
Section I: The Vocation, The Passion, The Desire	**13**
Quote 1: Measure Twice, Cut Once	15
Quote 2: Transforming the Raw into the Remarkable	16
Quote 3: From Humble Beginnings to Remarkable Creations	17
Quote 4: Turning Mistakes into Masterpieces	18
Quote 5: Symphony of Patience, Precision, and Passion	19
Quote 6: Harmony with Nature	20
Quote 7: Creating a Lasting Legacy	21
Quote 8: Design Opportunities, Not Mistakes	22
Quote 9: The Beauty of Personal Effort	23
Quote 10: Uncovering Hidden Potential	24
Section II: Tools of the Trade	**27**
Quote 11: Using the Right Tools	30
Quote 12: Mastery Through Tools	31
Quote 13: Tools as Extensions	32
Quote 14: Tools Reflecting Values	33
Quote 15: The Impact of the Right Tool	34
Quote 16: Tools Beyond Physical Objects	35

Quote 17:	Treasures of a Craftsman	36
Quote 18:	Tools Beyond the Physical	37
Quote 19:	The Spirit of Tools	38

Section III: Recycle, Reinvent, Rejuvenate   **41**

Quote 20:	Finding Beauty in the Discarded	43
Quote 21:	Rediscovering Purpose Amidst Wear and Tear	44
Quote 22:	Embracing Imperfections as Part of Your Story	45
Quote 23:	Crafting a Masterpiece from Life's Past	46
Quote 24:	Recognizing the Potential in Every Day	47
Quote 25:	Cultivating Patience in Woodworking and Life	48

Section IV: The Woodpile   **51**

Quote 26:	Elevating your work	52
Quote 27:	Preparation before Execution	53
Quote 28:	Reversing & Adapting the Process	54
Quote 29:	Nature & the Human Spirit	58
Quote 30:	Two Most Important Days	59
Quote 31:	Planting & Planning	60

Section V: Final Quotes   **63**

    Quotes from Bob Proctor   63

Conclusion: **68**

ACKNOWLEDGEMENTS

To my wife, Kris, for her support in this "Right Turn" I'm taking with my life.

To Craig Duswalt for making me see that something that I've thought about for years, and false started numerous times, is doable and achievable.

https://craigduswalt.com

To Mike Wolf for showing that it's never to late to follow your dreams.

https://mikewolfmastery.com

To Shopsmith® for providing me with the enjoyment and frustration of my initial woodworking attempts. https://www.shopsmith.com

And in memoriam, to Bob Proctor for starting me on this path. His talks, presentations, and books are what kick started me on this journey.

https://www.proctorgallagher.institute

PREFACE

Taking Control of Retirement and Redefining Life

Welcome to my journey, a journey that defies the traditional notions of retirement. I'm here to help those who are near retirement age but aren't ready to hang up their hats just yet, those who desire to take control of their lives and continue making a meaningful contribution to the world.

Who Am I?

I've traversed the milestones of the traditional retirement age and, instead of stepping back, I've stepped forward into a new career and life. My life's tapestry is woven with diverse accomplishments and experiences:

<u>Education:</u>
- From filling potholes and plowing snow to embarking on an entrepreneurial adventure, I've embraced the unconventional.
- At the age of 58, I earned my BSBA, proving that age is just a number when it comes to pursuing knowledge.
- With over thirty years of experience, I hold a PMP (Project Management Professional) certification.
- My heart still beats to the tunes of my generation's music, proving that some things never go out of style.
- I've earned a "Ph.D." in life from the school of learning from my mistakes.

Work History:
- I've served as a dedicated full-time Police Officer, ensuring the safety of my community.
- My commitment extended to being a Reserve Deputy Sheriff.
- I've been a part of an esteemed international consulting firm, working on complex projects.
- My journey led me to a small boutique consulting company.
- I've even dabbled in the world of software, adapting to the ever-evolving tech landscape.

Work-Life Balance:

For much of my life, work-life balance was an elusive concept.

As an employee, I had little control over my destiny, merely working for a paycheck. Even as an independent consultant, I was at the mercy of my clients' needs.

Now, I have the opportunity to create significance, make a difference, and set my own path.

Age doesn't dictate my journey; my desire, enthusiasm, and energy do.

Other Info:

I'm an only child, which instilled independence in me from a young age.

As a service brat, I moved every three years, adapting to new environments.

I'm not just a professional; I'm a husband, a father, and a proud grandfather.

I'm becoming who I want to be, not who I'm expected to be.

My Philosophy:

I don't dwell on why something can't happen; I focus on how to make it happen.

I live life through my eyes, not through the expectations of others.

My journey is a testament that retirement doesn't mean the end; it's a new beginning.

Join My Journey:

When you desire to control your life and continue to contribute, I'm here to guide you. My journey from near retirement to saying "Hell No" and embracing a new career and life is a testament that you can too.

I possess everything you need to navigate this journey with grace:

- Embracing getting older without succumbing to being "old."
- Staying deeply engaged in life.
- Remaining pertinent and valuable in a world that often overlooks experience.

Together, we can redefine retirement and show the world that age is just a number. So, let's embark on this journey together, because it's easier to learn from others' experiences and create the life you desire.

INTRODUCTION

In the world of woodworking and craftsmanship, there exists a treasure trove of wisdom that extends far beyond the workshop. These disciplines teach us about patience, creativity, resilience, and the transformative power of effort and dedication. The principles of woodworking are, in many ways, a metaphor for life itself. In this book, we embark on an enriching journey to explore a collection of quotes that draw profound parallels between woodworking and life. These insights will not only inspire but also guide you on your personal journey to fulfillment and success.

Many of the quotes presented are authored by Anonymous. Not sure who that is, but the wealth of knowledge bestowed on we mere mortals by that one individual can never be measured.

Each quote provides a unique insight and actionable advice, guiding us to embrace the art of repurposing in both woodworking and personal growth, ultimately encouraging them to find beauty and meaning in every aspect of their lives.

DON'T RETIRE ... REGROUP!

Knowledge is understanding the **Who & What** in our lives. Simply, the **Learning Process**.

Intelligence is understanding **How & Why** to apply our **Knowledge**,

Wisdom is understanding **When & Where** to apply our **Intelligence**.

SECTION I

The Vocation, The Passion, The Desire

"What you do for a living" and "your vocation" are related concepts, but they have distinct meanings and nuances:

What You Do for a Living:
This phrase refers to your occupation or job, the means by which you earn money to support yourself and your lifestyle.

It often emphasizes the practical or financial aspect of your work, focusing on the necessity of earning income to meet your basic needs and sustain your life.

Your Vocation, Passion, Desire:
Your vocation is a broader and more profound concept. It encompasses not only your occupation but also your calling or a sense of purpose in life.

Your vocation is often associated with a deep passion or sense of fulfillment that goes beyond simply earning a paycheck. It reflects what you believe you were meant to do or your higher purpose.

It may or may not align with your actual job. Some people are fortunate enough to have their vocation and occupation aligned, while others may find their vocation through volunteer work, hobbies, or other non-professional pursuits.

Your vocation can also be related to your values, beliefs, and the impact you want to make on the world. It's often more focused on personal fulfillment and self-expression.

In summary, "what you do for a living" is a straightforward reference to your job and how you earn a living, while "your vocation" is a deeper and more meaningful concept that encompasses your life's purpose, passions, and values, which may or may not be fully realized in your occupation.

Quote 1

Measure Twice, Cut Once

"Measure twice, cut once."
– Anonymous

This timeless woodworking adage serves as our initial guide in our exploration of the intersection between woodworking and life. It underscores the importance of careful planning and consideration before taking action in any aspect of life. We delve into the profound wisdom of thoughtful preparation and how it can lead to more deliberate and fruitful decision-making.

Great advice that is seldom taken. Hence the title of this book "Measure Once, Cut Twice." We all tend to rush into to things without taking the proper time and steps to ensure success. This also bring to mind the quote from Samuel Smiles that "We learn wisdom from failure much more than from success. We often discover what will do, by finding out what will not do; and probably he who never made a mistake never made a discovery."

This quote lays the foundation for the transformative journey ahead.

Quote 2

Transforming the Raw into the Remarkable

"Woodworking allows you to take a raw, natural material and transform it into something of lasting beauty and utility."
- Fine Woodworking Magazine

This quote reminds us of our innate capacity to transform the raw materials of our lives, such as skills, experiences, or resources, into something valuable and enduring. We explore the art of transformation and the creative process that turns the ordinary into the extraordinary.

Quote 3

From Humble Beginnings to Remarkable Creations

"The best thing about woodworking is that you get to create something beautiful and functional from a simple piece of wood."
– Anonymous

This quote introduces us to the incredible potential hidden within simplicity. It reminds us that, even from the most unassuming origins, we possess the ability to create something remarkable in life. We explore the transformative power of determination, creativity, and resilience. Just as a piece of wood can be shaped into a work of art, so too can we craft our lives into extraordinary works of meaning and purpose.

Quote 4

Turning Mistakes into Masterpieces

"A good woodworker knows how to hide their mistakes, but a great woodworker knows how to turn them into masterpieces."
– Unknown

In life, we inevitably encounter setbacks and make mistakes. This quote teaches us to embrace these experiences as opportunities for growth and innovation. We delve deep into the art of resilience, adaptability, and the importance of viewing challenges as steppingstones to greatness. By learning from our errors, we can, like skilled woodworkers, transform our lives into masterpieces of personal and professional achievement.

Quote 5

Symphony of Patience, Precision, and Passion

"Woodworking is a symphony of patience, precision, and passion."
- David Linley

In this quote, we explore the symphony that is woodworking and how it relates to the pursuit of mastery in life. Patience, precision, and passion are the notes that compose this harmonious melody. We delve into the importance of cultivating patience, honing our attention to detail, and infusing our pursuits with unwavering passion. These qualities, like the fine-tuned instruments of an orchestra, lead us toward mastery and fulfillment.

Quote 6

Harmony with Nature

"To work with wood is to harmonize with nature."
– Unknown

This quote invites us to deepen our connection with the natural world and recognize the value of aligning our actions with the environment. Just as a woodworker respects the qualities of wood, we learn the benefits of respecting and aligning with the forces of nature. Discover how working in harmony with nature can lead to a more balanced and fulfilling life, in sync with the rhythms of the Earth.

Quote 7

Creating a Lasting Legacy

"Woodworking is not just about making things; it's about making things that will last for generations." – Anonymous

What legacy are we leaving behind in our journey through life? This quote prompts us to reflect on the lasting impact we can have and the importance of creating a legacy that endures beyond our time. We explore the concept of leaving a meaningful mark on the world and how craftsmanship extends far beyond physical creations.

Quote 8

Design Opportunities, Not Mistakes

"In the world of woodworking, there are no mistakes, only design opportunities." – Anonymous

This quote is a celebration of the power of perspective. It encourages a positive outlook on setbacks and challenges in life, viewing them not as failures but as opportunities for growth and innovation. We explore the transformative potential of adopting a growth mindset, a mindset that sees each obstacle as a stepping stone toward a more profound understanding of ourselves and our capabilities.

Quote 9

The Beauty of Personal Effort

"The true beauty of woodworking lies in the journey of creating something with your own hands." – Unknown

Our journey takes a turn inward in this quote, where we underscore the intrinsic value of personal effort, craftsmanship, and the profound satisfaction that comes from creating something meaningful. We discover that the process itself, the journey of personal growth and self-discovery, is where the true beauty of life resides.

Quote 10

Uncovering Hidden Potential

"Every piece of wood has a spirit, and it is up to the woodworker to find and release it." - Chris Pye

Just as skilled woodworkers uncover the hidden potential within each piece of wood, we, too, can discover the untapped potential within ourselves and our circumstances. This quote serves as a guide in maximizing our potential and harnessing the latent energy within us to create remarkable outcomes.

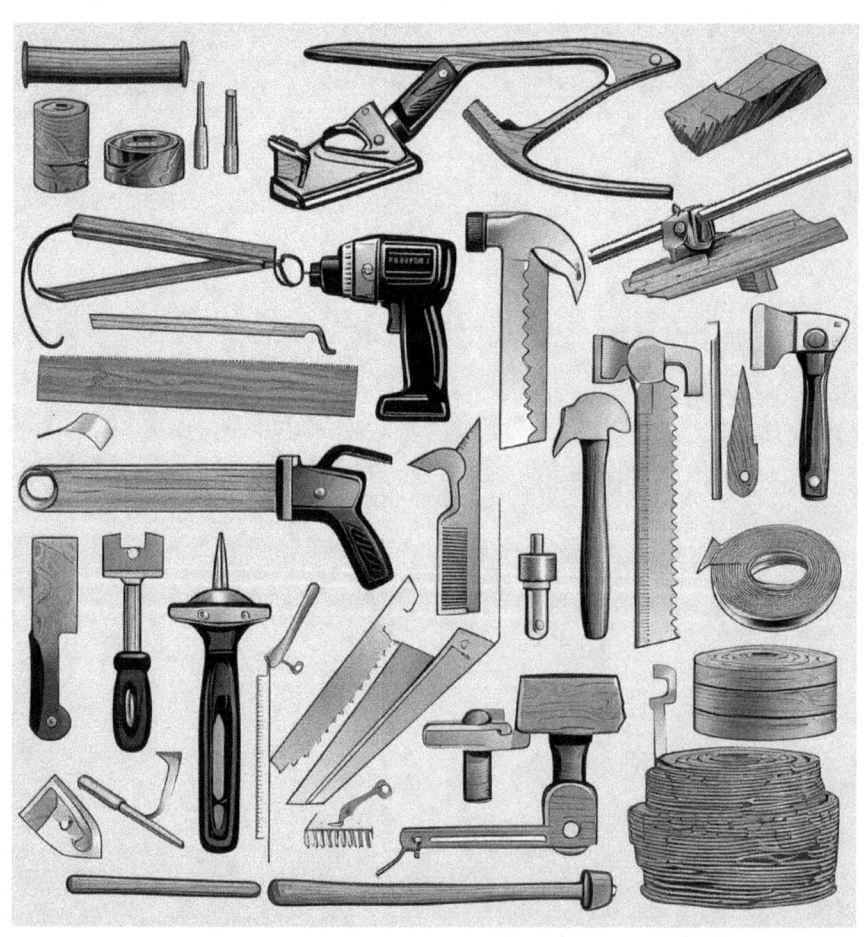

SECTION II

Tools of the Trade

"Tools of the trade" refers to the specific tools, equipment, instruments, or resources that are essential for a particular profession, occupation, or craft. These tools enable individuals to perform their job effectively and efficiently. The tools can vary widely depending on the field or industry. Here are some examples of tools of the trade in various professions:

Carpentry:
- **Hammer**: Used for driving nails and shaping materials.
- **Saw**: Various types like handsaws, circular saws, and jigsaws for cutting wood.
- **Chisels**: Used for carving and shaping wood.
- **Measuring Tape**: Essential for accurate measurements.
- **Wrenches**: Tools for tightening or loosening nuts and bolts.
- **Calipers**: Used for precise measurements.
- **Lathes and Milling Machines**: For shaping and cutting metal or other materials

Author

- **Paper & writing tools: To** Used for driving nails and shaping materials.
- **Word Processor**: To put your thoughts into a legible format and a basic format
- **Graphics**: Because a picture is truly often worth one thousand words.
- **Publisher**: To your manuscripts to put them into a format suitable for pulication

Cooking/Culinary Arts:

- **Chef's Knife**: A versatile knife for chopping and slicing.
- **Cutting Board**: Provides a safe surface for food preparation.
- **Mixing Bowls**: Used for combining and mixing ingredients.
- **Oven and Stovetop**: Cooking appliances for preparing dishes.

Medical:

- **Stethoscope**: Used by doctors and nurses to listen to patients' heart and lung sounds.
- **Scalpel**: A surgical instrument for precise cutting.
- **Syringe**: Used for injecting medications or extracting fluids.
- **Thermometer**: Measures body temperature.

Painting/Artistic Fields:

- **Paintbrushes**: Various types and sizes for applying paint.
- **Canvas**: The surface on which artists create their artwork.
- **Palette**: Used for mixing and holding paints.
- **Easels**: Support for holding the canvas while painting.

Information Technology (IT):
- **Computer**: The primary tool for most IT professionals.
- **Software Development Tools**: Such as integrated development environments (IDEs) and code editors.
- **Network Analyzers**: Used for diagnosing and troubleshooting network issues.

Teaching/Education:
- **Textbooks and Curriculum**: Resources for teaching subjects.
- **Whiteboard/Chalkboard**: Tools for visual aids during lessons.
- **Classroom Supplies**: Pens, markers, and educational materials.

Photography:
1. **Camera**: The primary tool for capturing images.
2. **Lenses**: Different lenses for various photography styles.
3. **Tripod**: Stabilizes the camera for long exposure shots.
4. **Photo Editing Software**: Used for post-processing and enhancing images.

These are just a few examples, and there are countless other tools of the trade in various professions, each tailored to the specific needs and requirements of that field. Every trade and occupation has them.

The trick is to use the right tools for your trade and task. Don't use a hammer to screw in a nail.

Quote 11

Using the Right Tools

"Use the right tool for the job."
– Anonymous

These tool-related quotes remind us to approach challenges with the appropriate skills and resources, and to be resourceful in finding the best solutions. We explore the importance of using the right tools, both physical and metaphorical, in various life situations, recognizing that the right tool can make all the difference.

Quote 12

Mastery Through Tools

"A craftsman is only as good as his tools."
- Emmert Wolfe

Just as a craftsman relies on quality tools, in life, having the right skills, knowledge, and resources is crucial for success. This quote explores the symbiotic relationship between skill and the tools that facilitate it. We delve into the idea that our mastery is a reflection of the tools we acquire and utilize.

Quote 13

Tools as Extensions

"A tool is but the extension of a man's hand, and a machine is but a complex tool." - Henry Ward Beecher

This quote highlights the profound idea that tools, whether physical or metaphorical, are extensions of our abilities, empowering us to accomplish more. We explore how tools enhance our capabilities and open doors to new horizons.

Quote 14

Tools Reflecting Values

"The tool is an extension of the hand, and the hand is an extension of the heart." - Neil Peart

We delve into how the tools we choose to use are an expression of our values, intentions, and capabilities. This quote explores the alignment of tools with personal values, emphasizing that our choices reveal our hearts and intentions.

Quote 15

The Impact of the Right Tool

"The right tool can make a world of difference in the outcome of a task." - Ron Kaufman

Having the right knowledge, skills, or resources can significantly influence the outcome of any endeavor. This quote delves into the transformative power of using the right tools, showcasing how the selection of the right tool can elevate our achievements and change the course of our lives.

Quote 16

Tools Beyond Physical Objects

"A tool is anything that helps you do the work that you are doing, or anything that helps you do it better." - Marshall Rosenberg

In life, tools can be knowledge, skills, relationships, or any resource that aids in personal or professional development. We explore the vast array of tools at our disposal and how they contribute to our growth and success. This quote broadens our perspective on what constitutes a tool, highlighting the diversity of resources available to us.

Quote 17

Treasures of a Craftsman

"Tools are the real treasures of a craftsman."
- M.C. Escher

This quote emphasizes the value and appreciation of the resources and skills we accumulate throughout our lives. We explore the richness of our personal toolkit and recognize that our experiences and acquired skills are the true treasures of our journey.

Quote 18

Tools Beyond the Physical

"A tool can be a physical object like a hammer or a saw, but it can also be a skill, a technique, or a mindset." - Chris Guillebeau

This quote expands the definition of a tool, reminding us that skills, attitudes, and approaches can be just as valuable as physical implements. We explore the versatility of tools in personal growth and how they can shape our outlook and enhance our lives.

Quote 19

The Spirit of Tools

"Every tool carries with it the spirit by which it was created."
- Werner Karl Weisenberg

As our journey nears its conclusion, we reflect on the profound idea that every tool, physical or otherwise, carries with it a unique spirit and history. This metaphorical perspective suggests that each resource or skill we possess is imbued with its own potential and purpose. We explore the depth of this concept and how it relates to our personal and professional lives.

SECTION III

Recycle, Reinvent, Rejuvenate

"Recycle," "reinvent," and "rejuvenate" are related concepts that all involve some form of transformation or renewal, but they have distinct meanings and applications

- **Recycle:**
    - Recycling is a process that involves converting waste materials into reusable materials. It is primarily associated with environmental sustainability.
    - In recycling, materials like paper, plastic, glass, and metal are collected, processed, and turned into new products rather than being discarded as trash.
    - Recycling aims to reduce the consumption of new resources, energy, and pollution by reusing existing materials.

- **Reinvent:**
    - To reinvent means to change or transform something significantly, often by introducing new ideas, concepts, or approaches.

- o It can refer to the process of taking an existing product, service, or concept and giving it a fresh, innovative twist to make it more relevant, appealing, or effective.
- o Reinvention is commonly associated with businesses and individuals who adapt to new challenges or trends by fundamentally changing their strategies or identities.

- **Rejuvenate:**
  - o Rejuvenation refers to the restoration or revival of something that has become tired, worn, or less effective. It involves making something or someone feel youthful or renewed.
  - o It can be applied to various aspects of life, including personal well-being, relationships, and physical or mental health.
  - o In a broader sense, rejuvenation can also refer to revitalizing a place or organization, making it more vibrant and energetic.

While these terms share a common thread of transformation or renewal, they differ in their specific focus and application. Recycling is primarily about sustainability and material reuse, reinvention pertains to making significant changes or improvements, and rejuvenation involves restoring or reviving something to a more youthful or vibrant state. Each concept serves a distinct purpose in different contexts.

Quote 20

Finding Beauty in the Discarded

"In woodworking, as in life, the beauty often lies in the repurposing of what others might discard."

Explore the concept that value and beauty can be found in overlooked or discarded aspects of life. Discover how to recognize the hidden potential in challenges, setbacks, and opportunities that others might dismiss. This quote encourages us to see their lives through the lens of a woodworker, transforming perceived limitations into sources of creativity and growth.

Quote 21

Rediscovering Purpose Amidst Wear and Tear

"Just like reclaimed wood, we can find new purpose and beauty in our own lives, even when we feel worn and weathered."

Delve into the idea that, despite life's hardships and the wear-and-tear of time, individuals can unearth fresh purposes and beauty within themselves. This quote provides practical guidance for rekindling motivation and finding significance even in the face of adversity.

Quote 22

Embracing Imperfections as Part of Your Story

"Every knot and imperfection in reclaimed lumber tells a story. Embrace your own imperfections; they are a part of your unique story."

Explore the profound insight that our imperfections and scars are essential components of our life narratives. Learn how to appreciate your individuality and the rich stories behind your own life's knots and blemishes. This quote empowers us to celebrate their unique experiences and personal growth journey.

Quote 23

Crafting a Masterpiece from Life's Past

"Woodworkers know that old wood can create new masterpieces. In life, our past experiences can be the foundation for creating something beautiful."

Discover how to use your past experiences as a foundation for crafting a fulfilling and beautiful future. This quote provides strategies for reflection, learning, and leveraging your history to create a unique and meaningful life masterpiece.

Quote 24

Recognizing the Potential in Every Day

"Woodworking teaches us that every piece has potential. Similarly, every day offers the chance to repurpose our time and make it count."

Learn to see the potential in each day of your life, just as woodworkers see potential in every piece of wood. This quote offers practical advice for making the most of your time, setting and achieving goals, and living with intention. It encourages us to transform ordinary days into extraordinary opportunities for personal growth and fulfillment.

Quote 25

Cultivating Patience in Woodworking and Life

"In woodworking, patience is key when repurposing wood. Likewise, patience can help us transform challenges into opportunities in life."

Explore the virtue of patience as it applies to both woodworking and life. Learn how patience can aid in navigating life's obstacles, uncertainties, and transformations with resilience and grace. This quote provides practical strategies for developing and applying patience in various aspects of life.

SECTION IV

The Woodpile

This section is more general. Much more loosely related to woodworking but still food for thought.

Quote 26

Elevating your work

"He who works with his hands is a laborer. He who works with his hands and his head is a craftsman. He who works with his hands and his head and his heart is an artist."
St. Francis of Assissi

The quote you've mentioned emphasizes the idea that the level of engagement, dedication, and passion put into one's work distinguishes different types of workers. Here's the life message encapsulated:

Your approach and attitude toward your work define your role and level of mastery. To truly excel and be an artist in your craft, you must invest not only your physical effort and skills but also your heart and passion into what you do.

This quote encourages individuals to go beyond mere physical labor (laborer) and even surpass the level of craftsmanship (craftsman) by adding a heartfelt connection to their work. It underscores the notion that when you genuinely love what you do and pour your emotions and creativity into it, you elevate your work to an artistic level. The message here is to strive for a deeper connection with your work, allowing it to become an expression of your passion and creativity, ultimately leading to a more fulfilling and meaningful experience in your chosen profession.

Quote 27

Preparation before Execution

"Give me six hours to chop down a tree and I will spend the first four sharpening the axe."
Abraham Lincoln

The quote, often attributed to Abraham Lincoln, conveys the importance of preparation, planning, and strategy in achieving a goal. The life message behind this quote can be summarized as follows:

Before embarking on any significant task or endeavor, invest time and effort in proper preparation and planning. By doing so, you can increase your chances of success and efficiency in the long run.

In essence, it encourages individuals to prioritize preparation and groundwork before taking on any major challenge. By spending time "sharpening the axe" in advance, you can make the actual task of "chopping down the tree" more effective and manageable. This message extends to many aspects of life, emphasizing the value of thoughtful preparation and the idea that investing time and resources upfront can lead to better outcomes in the future.

Quote 28

Reversing & Adapting the Process

"Woodworking requires a completely different kind of thinking and problem-solving ability than writing. With writing, you take a set of facts and ideas, and you reason your way forward to a story that pulls them together. With woodworking, you start with an end product in mind, and reason your way backward to the raw wood." ~ Joshua Foer

The comparison between woodworking and writing highlights the different approaches and problem-solving abilities required for these two activities. Here's a life application of this concept:

Adaptation and Versatility: This comparison between woodworking and writing can be applied to the idea of adaptability and versatility in life. It suggests that in various aspects of life, you may encounter situations where you need to employ different modes of thinking and problem-solving depending on the task at hand.

Recognizing the Task: Just as you recognize that woodworking and writing demand distinct approaches, in life, it's essential to identify what kind of problem or task you are facing. Is it more like woodworking, where you need to start with a clear end goal and work backward, or is it akin to writing, where you gather information and reason your way forward?

Flexible Thinking: Being adaptable and open to different thinking processes is a valuable life skill. Sometimes, you might need to be methodical and plan backward, as in woodworking. Other times, you might need to be creative and forward-thinking, as in writing. The ability to switch between these modes of thinking can be incredibly useful in both personal and professional contexts.

Balancing Approaches: Just as a skilled woodworker might occasionally use both forward and backward reasoning in a project, in life, you may find that a balanced approach combining different thinking styles can lead to better outcomes. Knowing when to plan meticulously and when to be creative can make you a more effective problem solver.

Continuous Learning: Both woodworking and writing require skill development and ongoing learning. Similarly, in life, it's essential to continually refine your problem-solving skills and adapt your thinking to different situations. Embracing lifelong learning can help you become more versatile and capable in various areas of life.

In essence, the life application of this concept encourages individuals to be adaptable thinkers, capable of recognizing which problem-solving approach is most suitable for a given situation and applying the appropriate mindset to achieve success.

Quote 29

Nature & the Human Spirit

There must be a union between the spirit in wood and the spirit in man. The grain of the wood must relate closely to its function. The abutment of the edge of one board to an adjoining board can mean the success or failure of a piece. () Gradually a form evolves, much as nature produces the tree in the first place. The object created can live forever. The tree lives on in its new form. The object cannot follow a transitory "style", here for a moment, discarded the next. Its appeal must be universal. Cordial and receptive, it should invite a meeting with man"
~ George Nakashima

The passage by George Nakashima emphasizes the deep connection between craftsmanship, nature, and the human spirit in the context of woodworking. Here's how this perspective can apply to life more broadly:

Holistic Connection with Nature: Nakashima's words encourage us to recognize and appreciate the profound connection between the natural world and our own existence. In life, this can remind us to be more mindful of our environment, to appreciate the beauty of the natural world, and to seek harmony with it.

Function and Form: The idea that the grain of wood must relate closely to its function highlights the importance of aligning purpose with design. In life, this can translate into making choices that are not only aesthetically pleasing but also functional and meaningful. It encourages us to find purpose and meaning in our actions.

Attention to Detail: Nakashima's mention of the critical role of the abutment of boards in the success or failure of a piece underscores the significance of paying attention to details. In life, this can remind us to be meticulous in our endeavors and to understand that small details can have a significant impact on the overall outcome.

Evolution and Adaptation: The idea of a form evolving, much like nature produces a tree, suggests the importance of adaptation and growth. In life, this perspective encourages us to embrace change and personal growth, recognizing that we can evolve and transform over time.

Timelessness and Universality: Nakashima's emphasis on creating objects that can live forever and have universal appeal speaks to the idea of creating things of lasting value. In life, this can inspire us to pursue endeavors that have enduring significance and to strive for actions and choices that resonate with people across time and cultures.

Authenticity and Invitation: The notion that objects should be cordial, receptive, and invite a meeting with people underscores the value of authenticity and openness in human interactions. In life, this can encourage us to be genuine in our relationships, welcoming to others, and open to meaningful connections.

Overall, Nakashima's philosophy in woodworking can be seen as a broader metaphor for how we approach life. It encourages us to connect with nature, align our actions with purpose, pay attention to details, adapt and grow, create things of lasting value, and be authentic and open in our interactions with others.

Quote 30

Two Most Important Days

"The two most important days in your life are the day you are born and the day you find out why."
Mark Twain

This quote carries a profound message about self-discovery and purpose in life.

The day you are born refers to the moment of your birth, the beginning of your existence. It signifies the first day of your physical life on this planet. However, it's important to note that merely being born does not inherently provide meaning or purpose to your life.

The day you find out when you discover your true purpose or calling in life. It represents the moment when you understand what gives your life meaning, what you are passionate about, and what you are meant to contribute to the world. It's a day of self-discovery and clarity about your life's mission.

In essence, this quote underscores the idea that life becomes truly meaningful when you discover and align with your purpose. It encourages individuals to explore and reflect on their passions, talents, and values to find their unique path and make a meaningful impact on the world. It serves as a reminder that life is not just about existing but also about finding and fulfilling one's purpose.

Quote 31

Planting & Planning

"The best time to plant a tree was 20 years ago.
The second best time is now."
Chinese Proberb

This quote is often attributed to a Chinese proverb, and it carries a powerful message about taking action and making positive changes in one's life.

"The best time to plant a tree was 20 years ago": This part of the quote emphasizes the importance of foresight and planning. It suggests that if you had taken action or made a decision 20 years ago, you would be reaping the benefits or enjoying the results of that action today. It underscores the idea that early action and long-term planning can lead to favorable outcomes.

"The second best time is now": This part of the quote is an encouragement to take action in the present moment. Even if you missed the opportunity to act or make a positive change in the past, the next best option is to start now. It implies that it's never too late to begin, and the present moment is the right time to take the first step toward a positive change or goal.

In essence, this quote urges individuals not to dwell on missed opportunities or past inaction but to focus on what they can do in the present to create a better future. It serves as a reminder that procrastination and hesitation can hinder progress, and the sooner one takes action, the sooner they can start seeing positive results.

SECTION V

Final Quotes

This section is dedicated to Bob Proctor. I've had the pleasure of listening to and reading his presentations. Although he is no longer with us, his thoughts and quotes are still thought provoking.

I've included them here without comment. I'm providing them to provoke thought and draw your own inspiration and motivation.

Quotes from Bob Proctor

"Strange thing about faith and fear: they both demand you believe in something you cannot see."

"Thoughts become things. If you see it in your mind, you will hold it in your hand."

"Be like a postage stamp. Stick to it until you get there"

"Set a goal to achieve something that is so big, so exhilarating that it excites you and scares you at the same time."

"Change is inevitable but personal growth is a choice."

"You are the only problem you will ever have and you are the only solution. Change is inevitable, personal growth is always a personal decision."

"Faith and fear both demand you believe in something you cannot see. You choose!"

"Most people are not going after what they want. Even some of the most serious goal seekers and goal setters, they're going after what they think they can get."

"You don't decide what your purpose is in life you discover it. Your purpose is your reason for living."

"A mentor is someone who sees more talent and ability within you, than you see in yourself, and helps bring it out of you."

"The only limits in our life are those we impose on ourselves."

"If you do not get the chills when you set your goal you're not setting big enough goals."

"The Subconscious mind cannot tell the difference between what's real and what's imagined."

"Do you want to know what you think about most of the time? Take a look at the results you're getting. That will tell you exactly what's going on inside."

"The only competition you will ever face
is with your own ignorance."

"Money is only used for two things. One, it's to make you comfortable, and the more comfortable you are the more creative you will become. And the other purpose is it enables you to extend the service you provide far beyond your own presence."

"Your purpose explains what you are doing with your life. Your vision explains how you are living your purpose. Your goals enable you to realize your vision."

"If you know what to do to reach your goal,
it's not a big enough goal."

"Everything has been created twice once on a mental plain and once on a physical plain."

"It doesn't matter where you are, you are nowhere compared to where you can go."

"You want to make sure that your purpose is something people can benefit from long after you're gone."

"No amount of reading or memorizing will make you successful in life. It is the understanding and application of wise thought that counts." -Bob Proctor"

"Everything you are seeking is seeking you in return therefore, everything that you want is already yours. It is simply becoming more aware of what you already possess."

"Discipline is giving yourself a command and following it up with action"

"If it's not broken, tinker with it till you find out how it works."

"When you really want something, and you couple that with an understanding of your nature, of your spiritual being, and the law that govern you, you will keep going, regardless of what's happened. Nothing will stop you."

"Wake Up Winners are wide awake; they are alive. Every day you will find them in the marketplace making things happen. The real winners are not just dreamers. Although they have dreams, they are doers: They realize their dreams. They are the bell ringers, always attempting to wake others up to the numerous opportunities life offers. If"

"I treat winning and losing exactly the same. I see them both as necessary steps to get us where we are going. Big failures big lessons little failures little lessons."

"All of the great achievers of the past have been visionary figures; they were men and women who projected into the future. They thought of what could be, rather than what already was, and then they moved themselves into action, to bring these things into fruition."

"You are not your job. It does not define who you are or all that you have to offer. Your real value is based upon who you are, not what you do. The only thing you need to do is express your real self to the world. You've been conditioned to think this is unproductive or that you can't make money at it. But you'll never know true happiness and fulfillment until you find the courage to do it anyway. Learn to trust your inner wisdom, even if the whole world says you're wrong"

"Part of our problem is that we use the term "decision" so loosely that it has come to describe our wishes, not our commitments. Instead of making decisions, we state our preferences. The word "decide" comes from the Latin decidere—the roots de-, meaning "off," and caedere, meaning "to cut"—therefore, making a decision means cutting off from any other possibility. A true decision, then, means you are committed to achieving a result, and then cutting yourself off from any other possibility."

"Persistence is a unique mental strength; a strength that is essential to combat the fierce power of the repeated rejections and numerous other obstacles that sit in waiting and are all part of winning in a fast-moving, ever-changing world."

CONCLUSION

"Measure Once, Cut Twice" has taken us on a profound journey through the intersections of woodworking and life. It has been a testament to the idea that even in the face of frustration and unexpected outcomes, there is wisdom to be gained.

Our exploration has revealed that, like a woodworker refining their craft over time, we too can refine our approach to life. We learn from our mistakes, embrace challenges, and ultimately create something remarkable from the simplest of beginnings.

This book has been a call to action, a reminder that our lives are works of art in progress, and we are the master craftsmen. Each quote has unveiled new facets of wisdom and inspiration, encouraging us to take ownership of our pursuits, to infuse passion and precision into our actions, and to use the right tools to shape our destinies.

As we conclude this portion our journey, let's carry forward the lessons learned from the world of woodworking and craftsmanship, knowing that our lives are the canvases upon which we create our own masterpieces.

Let's measure twice, cut once, and continue to explore the transformative power of effort and dedication, for it is in this journey that we find the true measure of our existence.

www.ingramcontent.com/pod-product-compliance
Lightning Source LLC
LaVergne TN
LVHW051911060526
838200LV00004B/89